CALLED!

CALLED!

Memoirs of a Black Priest

The Reverend Dr. Richard Cornish Martin

CHAPEL HILL

FULL-SERVICE
1970

BOOK-MAKERS
1998

PRESS

To all who recognized and supported Fr. Martin's
calling to serve the Lord, and especially to
those who comforted him in his final days.

CONTENTS

FOREWORD

The Rev'd Richard Cornish Martin honored Nashotah House Theological Seminary by accepting from her the degree of Doctor of Divinity *honoris causa* in 2012, having been an exemplary pastor and having served Nashotah many years as a most worthy trustee. When Fr. Martin knelt to receive that honorary degree, he had been a priest for fifty years. It is no exaggeration to say he was one of the finest of his generation.

Not the least reason for Fr. Martin's all-around excellence as a priest is that he was *called by the Lord* to the office and ministry of the priesthood and, as his memoir illustrates so ingenuously, called to every post he ever held in the Church. The true story of Richard's life is of being called to something while not looking for it or even looking in another direction. Read his testimony and see. Some episodes are so surprising they are funny. Some are wonderfully upending. I was honored to be an instrument in two of his calls—to the Church of the Advent, Boston; and to join me, after his retirement, at Saint Thomas Church Fifth Avenue in New York City. The key is, never once did Richard go seeking for a job. On the contrary, someone was always saying, "Excuse me, but would you please come to us and . . . ?"

The call to be Rector of St. Paul's, K Street, in Washington, DC, which Richard describes with beautiful understatement, is worth emphasizing here. In that call, Fr. Martin was asked, to the best of my knowledge, to become the first African American Rector of a predominantly white, notable, and affluent Anglo-Catholic parish. And yet, important as a racial milestone such an event would appear to be, the call to St. Paul's was far more a tribute to Richard Martin's known commitment to Anglo-Catholic orthodoxy and devotion, to his *gravitas* as a priest and pastor, to his theological knowledge and—let me just say it—to his genuine holiness.

We all cherish memories of this great priest. This one gets at the heart of why I love and miss him. As I sat in the Rector's Stall at Saint Thomas in New York, watching Fr. Martin preach, he was appealing with all his heart to Jesus, and suddenly turned to face the memorial 9/11 medieval crucifix next to the pulpit and gestured toward the Lord with open arms. *"Look at how much he loves us!"* Richard cried out.

Lovable, gentle, and wise; persevering and quietly stubborn when necessary; always orthodox and yet charitable toward all; scholarly; deeply reverent, and yet gifted with a fine sense of humor; kind and sympathetic; and above and in all utterly dedicated to Jesus—Fr. Richard Martin goes to the Lord riding on the wings not only of angels but of our love and prayers and grateful affection. May he rest in the peace of Christ and rise with him in glory.

The Rev'd Andrew C. Mead, OBE, DD
Rector Emeritus, Saint Thomas Church, New York City
The Feast of Candlemas, 2016

Father Mead with Father Martin

INTRODUCTION

When asked by Fr. Andrew Mead, the twelfth rector of St. Thomas Church, Fifth Avenue, to share some afterthoughts on ministry and priesthood, after almost fifty years in Holy Orders, it struck me that every aspect of ministry had been experienced as one of call. That was a surprise, as I had never sought nor applied for positions in the church. And so I begin, as it were, from the beginning.

THE CALL TO THE PRIESTHOOD

I was born in 1936 and reared in Philadelphia and was baptized in my first year by the archdeacon of Philadelphia, the Venerable Henry Laird Phillips, in the family home. He was also parish priest of the family church, the Church of the Crucifixion.

In addition to our connections with the Episcopal Church, the family was also influenced by Christian Science, so as a young child I attended St. Barnabas Church, Germantown, as well as Sunday school at the Second Church of Christ Scientist.

Other family members also attended, though not my mother. She and I were confirmed together by the bishop of Pennsylvania in 1954. So began activity in the Episcopal Church as acolyte and thurifer. Being a musician—piano and organ—I frequently played the organ, not only at St. Barnabas, but also for my organ teacher at his Baptist

Parents Leon and Virginia Martin

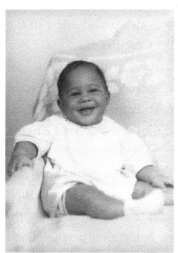

Growing up in Philadelphia

Enjoying his favorite pastime

*Serving as an acolyte at St. Barnabas
Episcopal Church, Philadelphia*

At Central High School, Philadelphia

Graduation from Penn State University

church. The seed of vocation was no doubt planted during these years before university.

From my earliest years I was interested in veterinary medicine, so my major at Pennsylvania State University was pre-veterinary medicine. My parents always encouraged me to keep up with music, and on my first Sunday in State College, I attended St. Andrew's Church. Whilst being greeted by the rector and the chaplain, I inquired if I could use the church organ to practice. Their response was, "We need an organist!" I was hired and appeared at the choir rehearsal. Thus began three years of working my way through college, doing what I loved. That was indeed a surprise call.

A sense of vocation was nourished by encouragement and support not only by the Episcopal priests but also a Presbyterian chaplain. Being in the Canterbury Club and the University Christian Association, others also encouraged me to consider the priesthood. Fr. Whitney, now rector of St. Andrews, took me to the Episcopal Theological Seminary in Virginia for a conference on ministry. That began the process of becoming a postulant in the Diocese of Pennsylvania, and though accepted by Bishop Oliver J. Hart, the rector of St. Andrew's wanted to sponsor me for seminary and ordination, as did the bishop of Harrisburg

(Central Pennsylvania). Thus, my postulancy was transferred, and St. Andrew's, State College, became my parish. The rector also stated that the parish would sponsor for ministry someone they themselves would welcome as their priest. All of this meant changing majors and graduating with a bachelor of arts degree in science. Virginia Theological Seminary (Alexandria, VA) offered to Black candidates a Bishop Payne Scholarship, making them beneficiaries of the merger of the prominently Black seminary in Petersburg with Virginia.

Whilst in seminary I was able to continue using my musical talents, not only assisting the seminary organist but playing often at the Meade Memorial Church in Alexandria. I also played for a Protestant service at a childre[n] center in Maryland.

All students are required to do fieldwork. I had atte[nded] St. Paul's, K Street, Washington, and found a home indeed. The rector, Fr. Richards, had a policy that he always choose as seminarian assistant the perso[n who] showed the most interest in St. Paul's. He never me[t] any other qualification.

When the seminarian assistant graduated, Fr[.] followed his established policy, and I was asked [to do my] education at St. Paul's. A true call. I never aske[d] but simply participated, and thus began a very [long associa]tion with St. Paul's.

UNEXPECTED CALL FROM HARRISBURG

Most seminarians do not know their immediate future after ordination until the middle of their senior year. But in April of my Middler Year, I was summoned to Harrisburg, having no idea what the bishop had in mind, other than I had indicated to him that I been chosen to attend the International Student Christian Association conference in Strasbourg, France, and needed funds, as well as his permission, since one's second summer in seminary was at the bishop's discretion, and I was given a tremendous opportunity. When I arrived in Harrisburg, my summer plans were not his first concern. He and my rector had been in communication, and his first question was, "Would you consider being Episcopal chaplain at Penn State?" I guess I was speechless, and he was obviously anxious for an answer. I think my reply was, "Sir, if that is what you want." I remember his sigh of relief. He said that

Fr. Whitney had refused to call a new chaplain, awaiting my ordination. That was a call indeed, totally unexpected. I was never unaware of the issue of race, but proceeded with God's grace and direction. I arrived back at the seminary, knowing my future, but careful to say nothing. The bishop then said, "About this summer…" He was very supportive, seeming proud that I was going to a world ecumenical conference, also my very first trip to Europe.

Ordained to the diaconate by the bishop of Harrisburg in June 1961, in St. Andrew's Church, State College, I arrived early in July and began organizing and planning for the fall semester, as well as adjusting to the role of deacon in the church of God. For many years I regarded St. Mark's, Locust Street, Philadelphia, as a kind of home, and so I was overjoyed when the rector, Fr. Emmett Paige, invited me to St. Mark's the first Sunday after ordination. There are many firsts in new beginnings—first car, first residence, first functioning alone, first sermon—a lot of firsts.

It was the custom at Penn State that the various chaplains be assigned an office in one of the residence areas, but we would also rotate, sharing our offices to be available to the whole campus.

We had the support of Penn State's official chaplain and the administration. We also had access to those students and faculty who indicated their religious preferences and were able to communicate with them. Having been a student and active in various aspects of campus life, I was known by many and became a part of the team. I was assigned the newest residence hall, East Hall, and my office was well-positioned because every student had to pass by it to get to the dining room and their mail. It was important that the Episcopal tradition have a significant presence and ministry. We began immediately with services in the Eisenhower Chapel, and we provided two buses on Sundays to gather students from all over the campus for services at St. Andrew's.

The local parish and campus ministry were one. As an assistant in St. Andrew's, I also had an office in the parish house. With the help of the parish secretary and that list of Episcopalians, I was able to develop the idea of meeting every single student, beginning with freshmen, so that at the end of three or four years, I might have contacted each student at least once.

I was ordained to the priesthood on January 13, 1962, and immediately began a daily Eucharist in the campus chapel. Eisenhower Chapel was shared by Roman Catholics, Lutherans, Anglicans, Quakers, and others. A strong group of students and faculty supported and attended. One evening a week (Wednesday), at the unusual hour of 9 p.m., we even celebrated a Sung Mass. For many students, especially graduate students, that was their main service of the week, leaving Sunday for study.

In the midst of the third year, a call from the chairman of the College Work Department of the Diocese of Washington—who happened to be the rector of St. Paul's, K Street—inquired if I would consider being the first full-time Episcopal chaplain at George Washington University. I had not considered leaving Penn State so soon, so I initially declined. A few months later, the rector called again and asked if I would reconsider. To that I said yes, and I journeyed to Washington to meet the suffragan bishop, Dr. Paul Moore, and learn more about what was expected at GWU. I then left for my second trip to England, to study at St. Augustine's College, Canterbury. One Sunday afternoon I was told that I had a transatlantic phone call

While Chaplain at George Washington University, Washington, DC

from Washington. It was Fr. Richards, who said that I had been chosen as chaplain, not only by the bishop of Washington, but by the president of the university! What's more, I would serve as assistant at St. Paul's and occupy the curate's apartment. Whilst I hesitated, he added, "Your apartment is air-conditioned." I said, "I'll take it!" Another genuine call! I had no idea I would end up in the nation's capital. I returned to State College, submitted my resignation, preached a last sermon, and began preparations to move.

When arriving in Washington at the end of the summer I was confronted with a great sadness and challenge. The president of George Washington University had died suddenly, and whatever he had in mind for this chaplaincy died with him. People knew I was coming, but then they did not know quite what to do. So we improvised.

I was given a desk in the Religion Building, and that was it. We had the essentials: a chaplain and several hundred Epis-

copal students, but no office and no meeting space, except what could be borrowed. But we did have the support of St. Mary's Church on 23rd Street, which was practically on the GW campus. St. Paul's Church was but a block or so away, and on many Sundays, students came for services. GWU was mainly a commuter university, with few dormitories, and students came from all over the Washington area. Thankfully, I had the support of a history professor

Always happy with children, especially on baptismal days

Left to right: Fr. Richard C. Martin,
Fr. James R. Richards, and Fr. Donald Munson

and the deans of several colleges, and I began some ministry in the law school and medical school. Two Eucharists were celebrated each week in the lounge, using a simple table—most informal.

I always believed in the importance of communication. As we had done at Penn State, a monthly newsletter was sent to students and faculty. A group of students enjoyed writing and editing, reproducing and mailing the newsletter. That was done from St. Mary's. The newsletters were addressed by hand, and one of the addresses was 1600 Pennsylvania Avenue, as President Johnson's daughter Lynda was one of the students on the list. She even wrote a note saying how pleased she was with the Episcopal activities, even though she could not participate.

FULL-TIME AT ST. PAUL'S

The rector of St. Paul's, blessed by a devoted and competent group of volunteers, preferred having two curates (senior and junior) rather than a paid secretary. The position of senior curate became vacant, and he quickly asked if I would consider the position. He was under some pressure as a number of clergy wanted to be considered. He also explained that the position was like that of associate rector, with tenure—that is, I would stay on as long as I wanted to, and as long as he was rector. With a two-month trip to Europe pending, I said yes, and he proudly announced his choice to the parish.

The trip included study at St. Augustine's College, Canterbury, as well journeying with friends to Paris, Milan, Rome, Vienna, Venice, and back to England. Traveling a long time can become wearying, so I spent some time in monasteries and shrines to pray and rest. But it was good to return to Washington and to St. Paul's.

Newly arrived at St. Paul's K Street, Washington, DC

I was told we made history in the diocese, as it is unusual for a rector to nominate his curate for bishop. But Fr. Richards did just that. The diocese had agreed to elect a Black priest as suffragan bishop. To my surprise I was nominated, and more surprised by the amount of support I had. I knew I would not be elected, as the diocese elected Canon John Thomas Walker, then on the cathedral staff, and who would become bishop of Washington. This was truly an unexpected honor for one so young. The result of the election process meant that I was now well-known in the diocese, and I was elected to the prestigious Standing Committee. I think I served at least eight terms, most of them as secretary. Of course, this all led to greater involvement in the life of the diocese.

Early in the 1960s I had joined one of the Church's devotional societies, the Society of Mary. I had attended several annual meetings, not completely realizing how new the American Region was. It was a society in formation, but led by clergy and laity of such enthusiasm, vision, and commitment that I thought it was firmly established and with resources.

I had missed an annual meeting, usually held at St. Clement's Church, Philadelphia, in the month of May, so I was shocked and surprised by a phone call at the end of the summer, asking when the council was going to meet.

I am sure my response was, "What council?" and "How would I know?" Then I was informed, "You were

With The Right Revd. Arthur Michael Ramsey, Archbishop of Canterbury

elected Superior at the May meeting." No one had told me. Another surprise, another call.

One of the oldest and most venerable societies of priests in the Anglican Communion, the Society of the Holy Cross, was founded by fathers of the Oxford Movement in London in the mid-nineteenth century. Membership is by invitation only. In 1971 I was invited to become a member, as the secretary of the SSC (Societas Sanctae Crucis) was making his first visit to the United States. I do not remember details—who recommended me, or which chapter approved—but I remember being admitted on September 8 as the very first American so admitted in America. Other American members were admitted in England or Wales. Fr. Hinton moved on from Washington and admitted several others in New Jersey and Illinois. However, whenever in England I would attend meetings. Before long, an American Region grew to several hundred priests.

CALLED TO STAY IN WASHINGTON

Knowing that the rector of St. Paul's was planning retirement, I also knew I must move on. Where I did not know. Several calls came, but the bishop of Washington wanted me to stay, so I was asked if I would consider being rector of St. George's Church, located adjacent to Howard University. After meeting with the wardens and vestry, I was duly elected and began in September 1973. The Service of Institution was preceded by a community fair. In procession from the local school were over fifty priests and three bishops (in cope and mitre!). The church was new and architecturally unique and unusual. Its ministries to the youth and the elderly had a tremendous impact in the LeDroit-Bloomingdale area of the city, and included many students from Howard University and elsewhere involved in tutoring and mentoring. The church and local school worked closely together. Hundreds of children were touched by St. George's, especially its summer programs, staffed by youth employed by the city.

I took advantage of continuing education opportunities, especially the Canterbury Ecumenical Summer School (CANTESS) at Christ Church College, and Rome Ecumenical Summer School, which included lectures and visits to the Vatican. I was also well acquainted with the Anglican Centre in Rome, visiting there many times. The Society of Mary provided a Marian library at the centre, and for many

Installation day at St. George's—Fr. Martin with The Right Reverend William F. Creighton and The Right Reverend John T. Walker, Bishops of the Episcopal Diocese of Washington

years I gave the centre yearly subscriptions of the *Episcopal Church Annual*. The Anglican Centre in Rome invited Anglicans from all over the Anglican Communion to spend time in meetings and conferences at the centre, the Vatican, and other parts of Rome and Italy. Thus how surprised I was to receive an invitation to join an American delegation of some twelve bishops, priests, and laypersons. The wardens and vestry of St. George's were proud of such an opportunity and made the trip possible. The entire month of March was spent in Rome. This was another unexpected call.

As rector of the parish adjacent to Howard University, I thought it made sense to consider pursuing an advanced degree at the Howard University School of Divinity. The dean of the school was most encouraging, assuring me that many ministers studied whilst tending their congregation. As I did not intend on teaching, I did not need a PhD. I wanted a degree with a strong theological emphasis, rather than the emphasis on pastoral care that other seminaries offered.

I was determined to write a history of the American Region of the Society of Mary, as well as "Mary in the Episcopal Church." My academic supervisor understood exactly what I had in mind, and he guided me toward the doctor of ministry degree, which I received in 1988. Again, the wardens, vestry, and people of St. George's did everything to assist and support me, and I endeavored to neglect no part of parish ministry.

I spent sixteen years as rector of St. George's. I never sought episcopal election, but one never knows what God has in mind. Bur if there was a serious and sincere inquiry, it just may be a time for discernment. Two such calls came in the 1980s. The Diocese of Milwaukee prepared to elect, and I was on the ballot. I learned not to take things too seriously. Again, I did not expect to win, but I was deeply honored by such consideration.

The Diocese of Northern Indiana was seeking a new bishop, and I was told that a large group of clergy wanted me to be considered. The great surprise was that I had the clergy vote but not the laity, which meant I came in a very close second. Again I was deeply honored and grateful for the experience.

With best wishes to Richard Martin — Jimmy Carter

CALLED BACK

The year 1989 was a difficult year and a year of changes. Early in the year, one of the teenagers of St. George's was tragically killed. A month or so later, my father died. After Easter I journeyed to England for the International Congress of the Society of the Holy Cross. That was a healing experience. Early in May, the rector of St. Paul's, K Street, Fr. James Daughtry, announced his resignation. There had been conflicts between the rector/vestry and the bishop of Washington, with the bishop agreeing not to visit the parish for several years. It seemed best and appropriate for the rector to resign. Having served once before as a kind of consultant to the rector-search process, I was not surprised by a phone call from the chairman of the search committee to meet with them for Sunday lunch. The vestry did not want an interim or a long search process, as they were concerned about the fragile atmosphere in the parish, and they feared what the diocese might attempt to do. We met at a restaurant on the Virginia side of the Potomac, where no one we knew might appear. In the midst of the conversation, the chairman said that they wanted to ask me a question. Each member had come to the same conclusion on their own.

He asked, "Would you be our rector?" I was shocked into total silence. They indicated that the vestry members had apparently come to the same conclusion. I guess I left that luncheon numb and unbelieving. All of this was strictly "under the seal." Nobody was to know anything, and there must be no leaks. The following Tuesday evening I met with the vestry of St. Paul's in a private home; not even spouses were to know. The following Saturday morning after Mass, the vestry met to elect—that is, hold an election of intention. They would inform the bishop whom they wished to elect and, after the bishop's approval, would proceed to a formal election. The phone rang, and I had been unanimously elected. Then came the response from the bishop. The phone rang again. It was Bishop Walker. Not only did he approve, but he indicated that I was his very first choice as rector of St. Paul's, and then said, "You will accept, won't you?" I said, "Yes," and called the senior warden. Now began the process of notifying the respective congregations in such a way that all would receive the news at the same time

After Mass on Sunday morning I told my wardens and lay minister, and after many tears, an emergency vestry

Installation day at St. Paul's—Fr. Martin with The Right Reverend Sergio Carranza-Gomez, sixth Bishop of Mexico and former classmate at Virginia Seminary, and The Right Reverend Ronald H. Haines, Bishop of Washington DC

meeting was called to receive my resignation and communicate the news to St. George's. Both parishes arranged for letters to be sent on Tuesday so that all would receive the same news at the same time. I was now the eighth rector of St. Paul's–elect.

With several priests on the staff I was able to arrange arrival across town by the first of September, allowing time for things to get sorted out at St. Paul's, the vestry and people of St. George's to consider their future, and myself to enjoy a holiday.

I knew this would be a most difficult ministry, and I would ask the Lord, "Why me?" The bishop made it clear that I was to be healer and reconciler, and keep the parish together.

What would I say at my first sermon that would set the tone and vision for this ministry? What would be my motto? At St. George's, wanting the people truly to know and love the Lord and be informed as much as possible, I chose a text from the Apostle Paul: "Brethren, I would not have you ignorant."

Whilst traveling on a train in England, a text from St. John's Gospel came to mind: "Sir, we would see Jesus." That was the text for the first sermon of my rectorship. I had a conviction that by focusing on Jesus, we would downplay conflicts and troublesome issues and get on with the mission and unity of the church. People needed to see Jesus, in the Word proclaimed, in the Sacraments, and in the Christian community. It was indeed a tumultuous time, but not without accomplishments. And the parish, in spite of everything, was kept together, albeit with a few people feeling compelled to leave.

For many years I had served on the Standing Committee of the diocese, with a good portion of that time as secretary. For several years I decided to keep a low profile in the diocese. However, upon becoming rector of St. Paul's, I was asked to consider election to the Standing Committee again. Though I hesitated, it seemed best for St. Paul's and its position in the diocese that the eighth rector again assume a leadership position. To my surprise I was elected on the first ballot, and it was probably my eighth or ninth term—and a few years later, another term. It was important that St. Paul's not be alienated from the diocese, and to continue its unique and respected tradition.

Within that first year I was also elected to the board of trustees of Nashotah House Theological Seminary (Wisconsin).

I thought that episcopal elections were no longer to be a part of my life, but into my second year as rector, a call came from the Diocese of Chicago, which was planning on electing a suffragan bishop. After only one year I did not want the people at St. Paul's to think I was seeking further preferment, but I had to be sure about my decision, and the Diocese of Chicago had a short list of candidates. Members of the search committee arrived for a weekend, and though they worshipped at St. Paul's, they met with representatives from St. George's Parish to learn as much about me as

A kiss from Mother on this special day

possible. Then the call came that I was one of five finalists, and a visit to the Bishop of Chicago was arranged. I journeyed to the Windy City, truly seeking a sign. Time was of the essence, for in a few days the search committee would make its final report and distribute to the diocese four or five names. I arrived back in Washington with a distinct decision: God was not calling me to Chicago. I called the chairman of the committee and asked that my name be withdrawn. He was quite upset and tried to convince me that I had a good chance. I knew I had made the right decision. Once again, it was truly an honor to be considered, but I opted for a "K Street headache," not a purple one!

The entrances to St. Paul's had never been completed, and plans were afoot to build onto either side of the church as well as undertake extensive renovations. These ideas and plans went back many years, including my seminary days. Also, the organ needed serious attention. We began a massive capital fund campaign to begin a three-phase building and renovations program. The first phase was a new organ, and climate control of the church to protect it. The organ builder chosen was from San Francisco, the Schoenstein Company, which ultimately provided a showcase instrument on the East Coast. A splendid organ it is.

After seven tumultuous years I tested the waters of retirement by taking a sabbatical. I indicated to a few people that I would consider early retirement, but that I would rather continue in active ministry to be able to qualify for a new

Standing in the courtyard at St. Paul's

proposal to be approved by the General Convention: clergy over fifty-five years of age with thirty years in ministry could retire with full benefits. I had no idea whether I would return to St. Paul's or move on, but if I left, where would I go? It was then that the rector of the Church of the Advent, Boston, who had just been elected a rector of St. Thomas Church, Fifth Avenue, New York, asked if I would consider being in charge of the Church of the Advent. I received a call from the

senior warden and a visit from the junior warden. I then had an appointment with the bishop of Massachusetts and a meeting with the Advent's vestry. The bishop was supportive, and the vestry elected me, but with an interesting title: Vicar. Fr. Mead and his wife were poised to move to New York, and the vestry wanted it known

As Vicar at Church of the Advent, Boston

that the interim had indeed arrived in Boston and was in the rectory. Fr. Mead met me at the rectory door and handed me the keys to the church. How is that for smooth transition? Never in my wildest dreams would I have thought I would be at the great Church of the Advent, Boston—and for over three years. The situation at the Advent is a long and complicated story, regarding governance and several court cases. Wisely, the parish had been reduced (temporarily) to mission status, hence the title "vicar." When the legal battles were settled on behalf of the vestry and diocese, and the former corporation dissolved, parish status was restored, and I became interim rector. The process of electing a rector began.

I was over fifty-five years of age and a priest for over thirty years, and thus eligible to retire. That I did at the end of 1999. At the first Sunday for the new rector, Fr. Allan B. Warren, I was celebrant at an early Mass and he preached. But at the Solemn Mass, he was celebrant and preacher. Though sitting in choir for the first part of the Mass, I deliberately departed at the offertory, placed my keys on the administrator's desk, got into my car, and began the journey to Philadelphia, and then to a new residence in Columbia, South Carolina. It was truly Fr. Warren's day, and the beginning of a new chapter at the Church of the Advent.

I officially retired at the end of 1999 and moved to South Carolina to share a home with a nephew and see what it was like living in the South. During the fall, word leaked out to the bishop of South Carolina that I was moving to Columbia, and he called to ask if I would work with him in the Diocese of South Carolina. Once again, an unexpected call. Before the beginning of the new year I met with Bishop Salmon to find out what he had in mind. We had been friends since our time together at Virginia Theological Seminary. What he had in mind was my being interim rector of St. Mark's Church, Charleston. Over the years I had heard of St. Mark's and never dreamed I would have anything to do with it, or enjoy the lovely city of Charleston.

After meeting with the wardens and vestry, I began the weekly journey to celebrate and preach, and to give some assistance and guidance to the vestry. St. Mark's is one of the most beautiful churches in Charleston, with a distinguished history. Sadly it had declined from one of the largest congregations to about a hundred people. But we gathered Lord's Day by Lord's Day to build the community and pray for a new vision of mission and service.

After several years, my nephew and I decided to return "home"—that is, to the Washington or Philadelphia area. We decided to compromise and live in Baltimore, where property was indeed an investment. I had for many years been a priest associate of the All Saints Sisters of the Poor in Catonsville, Maryland, and now they asked me to be their chaplain general. I had known the Sisters since seminary days, and I participated on many retreats and enjoyed many visits with them. Now I was able to minister to them in a unique way, especially during a period of discernment when they wrestled with their future: whether to stay within the Episcopal Church or not.

Now there was another surprise call. The bishop of Pittsburgh called to ask if I would consider a project in his diocese. How could that be possible? I lived in Baltimore and was not about to move. The bishop had a vision of Grace Church, Mount Washington, Pittsburgh, being the center of an Anglo-Catholic mission, having some influence in western Pennsylvania. Grace Church was revived within the Catholic tradition, and unique in that it was one parish in two locations: the mother church in Pittsburgh and a daughter congregation, Grace Church, Edgeworth, near Sewickley. The Edgeworth congregation was in the midst of seeking a permanent location and temporarily worshiped in a Lutheran church in Sewickley on Saturday evenings. A furnished apartment was secured in Sewickley, and I journeyed each Saturday, either driving or flying, to spend the weekend. Grace Church was blessed with a staff of several priests and a deacon. One of the priests was also a banker, and he exercised his priesthood by being responsible for the Edgeworth congregation, whilst assisting on Sundays at Mount Washington. The other priest was also a lawyer, and he exercised pastoral care in the congregation, assisted by the deacon. Thus, the day-to-day work of the church was tended to, and my task was to teach, as well as to celebrate and preach. Grace Church is a lively, dynamic community within the Catholic tradition.

With nephew Dr. Stacey Settle, Spring, 1995

After several years my nephew and I were faced with an opportunity to move to Durham, North Carolina. My nephew had received a call to assist the provost at North Carolina Central University and teach. A splendid house was found, and I was able to retire again, But within a year, a call came from the rector of St. Thomas Church,

With sisters Fatimah Abdulahad and Dr. Leona Martin, 2014

Receiving an honorary doctoral degree from Nashota House, 2012

Fifth Avenue, New York. I was not about to move again. But he suggested we work something out. He had in mind having a relatively well-known, retired, Anglo-Catholic priest on the staff, albeit part-time— a kind of priestly presence. It sounded like being a "paid decoration," and I said, "I can do that." It was agreed that I would spend three weeks each month in New York, and a week at home in Durham. A furnished apartment was provided in the St. Thomas Choir School. I was on the rota for low Masses, occasional preaching and teaching, and just being available. I attended clergy staff meetings and, above all, was blessed by the splendors of St. Thomas: the marvelous liturgies, Evensong, and music that took one to the gates of heaven. To be invited to spend a few years in New York and at St. Thomas was a blessing indeed. After several years, an illness signaled the time to truly retire—or at least to stop having to journey so far.

The great joy of the priesthood is the celebration of the Mass, proclamation of the gospel, and teaching the full apostolic and catholic faith. And being invited to do just that is what I have been able to do at St. Timothy's Church, Raleigh, thanks to the rector, Fr. Jay James. I have also gladly helped out at St. Titus' Church, Durham.

From beginning to end, it has been one call after another—applying for nothing, searching for nothing, expecting nothing. It was always a surprise and a blessing, as well as an opportunity, to serve in places I would not have thought would call me. I look back in utter amazement, with a sense of tremendous joy and thanksgiving.

To the living and true God, the Father, the Son, and the Holy Spirit, be all honor, praise, and glory, now and unto the ages of ages. Amen.

THE REVD. FR. RICHARD CORNISH MARTIN, SSC, DMIN, DD

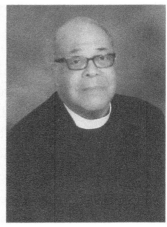

Fr. Jay James was a constant and loyal friend,
especially at the end of Fr. Martin's life

REVEREND DOCTOR RICHARD CORNISH MARTIN

Reverend Doctor Richard Cornish Martin, 78, died on June 27, 2015. Father Martin was born (1936) in Philadelphia, Pennsylvania. He was the son of the late Leon F. Martin and Virginia (Bullock) Martin. He graduated from the Central High School of Philadelphia, and received the Bachelor of Arts in Science from the Pennsylvania State University. He received the Master of Divinity from the Virginia Theological Seminary, and the Doctor of Ministry from the Howard University School of Divinity, Washington DC.

Continuing education included courses in England (St. Augustine's College), Wales (St. Deiniol's Library), and Jamaica (University of the West Indies). He was ordained to the Diaconate (1961) and to the Priesthood (1962) by the Bishop of Harrisburg (Central Pennsylvania).

Father Martin began his ministry as Episcopal Chaplain to the Pennsylvania State University and Associate Rector of St. Andrew's Church, State College, PA. He was called to the Diocese of Washington to serve as Episcopal Chaplain to the George Washington University, and Assistant at St. Paul's Parish - K Street, where he had been a seminarian assistant. He became Associate Rector of St. Paul's, and then as the third Rector of St. George's Parish, Washington. He was then called to return to St, Paul's as its Eighth Rector. Prior to retirement, he was interim Rector of the Church of the Advent, Boston, Massachusetts. In retirement, he has been Interim-Rector of St. Mark's Church, Charleston, SC; Interim-Rector of Grace Church, Pittsburgh, PA; and Assistant at St. Thomas Church, Fifth Avenue, New York. Most recently he served as Assistant at St. Timothy's Church, Raleigh. He was honored several times by nomination to the episcopacy (dioceses of Washington, Milwaukee, Botswana, and Northern Indiana).

In the Diocese of Washington he served over eight terms on the Standing Committee (six times as Secretary); the Commission on Ministry and was Editor of the Diocesan Cycle of Prayer. He was also founder of the Cathedral "Nave Clergy". He served on many committees and ad hoc commissions, including Peace and Justice, Liturgy and Music, the Diocesan Council, and Diocesan Court of Appeals.

His civic involvement included the DC Board of Professional Responsibility of the Court of Appeals; the Research Board of Childrens' Hospital; the Board of Directors of the Prevention of Blindness Society; and the Committee for Community Improvement, etc. He was for forty-six years, Superior of the Society of Mary (American Region), and served on the Council of the Guild of All Souls. He was the first priest admitted to the Society of the Holy Cross in the United States (1971) and served as Deputy Master. He served on the Board of Trustees of Nashotah House Theological Seminary. He was Founder and Convenor of the "Anglo-Catholic Rectors". He was a member of Societas Liturgica, and of the Anglican International Liturgical Consultation. On May 20, 2015, he was recipient of the Archbishop Arthur Michael Ramsey Medal and the Distinguished Alumni Medal from the Nashotah House Theological Seminary. He was a member of Viri Viginti of Philadelphia and of the Alpha Phi Alpha Fraternity, Inc.